Beyond Profit:

Touching the invisible in customer relationships

Leonardo Barci

Beyond Profit: Touching the invisible in customer relationships

Editor: Leonardo Dias Barci
Publisher responsible: Julie Anne Caldas
Review: Top Texto
Layout: Leonardo Dias Barci

**International Cataloging Data in Publication (CIP)
(Câmara Brasileira do Livro, SP, Brasil)**

Barci, Leonardo
By the original: Além do lucro: tocando o invisível no relacionamento empresa-cliente - São Paulo, SP, 2016.

1. Customers - Contacts | 2. Customers - Relationship | 3. Relationship Marketing | 4. Social media | 5. Customer Services | 6. Success in Sales

14-06700 - CDD-658.812

Index for systematic catalog:

1. Clients: Relationship Marketing: Business Administration 658,812
2. Customer Relationship Marketing: Business Administration 658,812

ISBN: 1986571823
ISBN13: 9781986571821

Copyright © 2016 Leonardo Barci
All rights reserved to the author.

No part of this book may be reproduced, copied, transcribed or even transmitted by electronic means or recordings, as well as translated, without the written permission of the author. Offenders will be punished by the Brazilian Law No. 9,610, dated February 19, 1998.

Leonardo Barci
leonardo@barci.com.br
(Brazil) +55 11 99 678 5475

To my grandmother, Isabel

To my mother, Fernanda

To my wife, Marianne

Inspired by the works of Eva **Pierrakos***

Eva was an Austrian medium, settled in the United States who channeled the teachings of a spiritual entity that were later compiled in The Pathwork Guide Lectures and constitute the foundations of Pathwork, a spiritual path of self-purification and self-transformation involving all levels of consciousness.

Her teachings on relationship came to the author Leonardo Barci as he went through a moment of searching for his inner happiness. "Over time, I realized that the key to what I sought to have in my relationship with others was to relate to my inner self. When we meet ourselves, we find the other and we can create a relationship of transcendence, peace and balance, whether in personal or professional life ", says the author.

SUMMARY

FOREWORD 9
INTRODUCTION 21
1 – WHAT IS A RELANTIONSHIP? 28
2 - WHY RELATE? 36
3 - WHAT IS NEEDED? 40
4 - HOW A RELANTIONSHIP BEGINS 46
5 - THE CHOICE TO GO AHEAD 58
6 - WHY DOES NOT WORK? 68
7 - HOW TO "FIX" IT 78
8 - IF THE RELANTIONSHIP IS REAL, SO HOW TO PERCEIVE IT 84
9 - HOW TO BE STRONG ENOUGH TO 'SUSTAIN' THE RELATIONSHIP 92
10 - "WHAT IF MY PAST CONDEMS ME?" 100
11 - HOW TO 'SOLVE' IT IF BECOMES TOO 'HEAVY' 107
12 - FROM NOW ON 115
13 - HOW TO PREPARE YOURSELF TO THE END 121
14 - HOW TO DANCE WITH LIGHTNESS 129
BEFORE WE GO 135

FOREWORD

THERE'S one thing that moves me, for which I'm totally in love, it's people! I love meeting different people, living a life different from mine, acquiring knowledge different from mine, learning languages that I do not speak, studying books that I have not even read. I love learning from people instead of reading books. And whenever I learn something new from someone, I feel like transmitting that knowledge to someone else. More than that, I would venture to say that this is my gift: to put into words someone's knowledge, information or experience, so that it can reach other people. I relate to people through words. And this way of relating to others has to do with how I came to edit this book.

I was 30 years old and undergoing a divorce and restructuring my company when I met Leo. Leonardo Barci, author of this book, was introduced to me by a mutual friend, Marcio Oliveira, who was in that year beginning to work at youDb, a company that Leo had built. We met with a reason: they - Leo and Marcio - experts in the subject *Relationship with Customers*, wanted to write a book about it; And I, on the other hand, had no marketing knowledge, but I know how to write. Journalist by training, I started my career as a sports reporter, but the paths took me to the pages of magazines, a vehicle in which I believe I graduated as a "writer of texts", a real storyteller. That's what I am. And also, passionate about absorbing knowledge and passing it on, remember? That's why I accepted the challenge that Leo and Marcio made to me at that time. Yes, challenge, because although I already have a beautiful collection of texts published in magazines, newspapers and websites, I had never written a book. They, in the other hand, trusted that I could do a good job and, more than that, they entrusted to me their precious knowledge.

The process of capturing the content happened through weekly conversations that we had for months. And it was at this period when I approached Leo. Anxious to pass on all the knowledge he had, he almost always curled up himself to explain what he was thinking, he could not turn into words what he really meant. But somehow, I still managed to catch it. "That!" he would say excitedly to hear me "deciphering" his ideas, and would almost always end with a laugh. And before every conversation, every meeting, I found myself anxious for what I would learn that day. So, between chatting, coffee, laughter and lots of learning, the book Mind The Gap was written and, a while later, published and released. Our work together worked out well. But something much bigger happened during this period: those conversations were for me one of the moments I learned most in my life - and this, for all the gratitude I showed them at the time of the book's release, perhaps Marcio and Leo do not know.

If nothing of what is written here in this preface, which Leo himself asked me to write, made sense to you so far, it is time to understand: the relationship that I, as a professional and entrepreneur, learned to have with my clients, Marcio and Leo, in doing the work of writing that first book, changed my way of looking at my professional life. I learned from them much more than they had imagined teaching me. I opened myself, as a professional and a person, to receive, to acquire, any and all, knowledge that they wanted to give me. I did not impose work rules. I did not write the book my way; I did it for them, thinking of them. I let the relationship with my client's flow.

So, the pride I felt at seeing the work done was without measure. Pride not only for my work done - which I learned to be important to feel as well - but for having learned from them, to see that I understood the so valuable lessons that they have passed me. Proud to say that I learned how a company should relate to its customers from the best ideas I've read or heard about it - and the most dedicated professionals I've ever met. No, I'm not a marketing expert. But "such a relationship with the client" had already dribbled in front of me many times (after all, I'm a businesswoman), without, however, having managed to get my attention. Because Leo and Marcio have succeeded, and the motive is one: instead of captivating with words, they look at the details in doing the best for their clients. And in that case, having a book that summarized everything they believed to be important to address about relationship was the goal to reach those clients. And they devoted themselves so much to this, to me, the result could not be other than having fully attained the goal. Except for one point: one book was not enough. Still good!

Months ago, when Leo came to me to say that I had another idea that I wanted to turn into a book, my first thought was, "Whatever the idea is, I'm sure it will make a great book." Well, that's until I heard him say about what it actually was: "I want to turn into a book some articles I've written about relationship with the client based on spiritual knowledge." Hello? "How could he have taken any learning from such a religious book? Is it not going too far?", I thought. No. For Leo, going beyond is never going too far. Because, for him, learning more is never too much; Being a better professional is never too much; Discovering how to relate even more fully to your customers is never too much; And above all, conveying all his marketing knowledge to others who are still starting is never too much. Lucky for me being the medium of this transmission.

In editing this book, I once again learned beyond the obvious. I have learned that when we are open to receive knowledge, it comes. Wherever it may be. I learned that everything we try to do in this earthly world - and that includes being successful as professionals and entrepreneurs - will not succeed unless we look at the spiritual world that is all around us and within us. As a matter of fact, by having access to all this knowledge, I still learned how I can improve my company's relationship with our clients. And even more so, I learned that I can be and do more and better through my marriage - yes, that divorce I quoted at the beginning of the text happened, but I got married again.

So, if by having access to this book you wondered if it will teach you how to create a good relationship with your customers to generate results for your company, the answer is: no; It is capable of much more than that. Despite the segmented name, Beyond Profit - Touching the invisible in customer relationships, is a true mirror that captures and deeply reflects not only the professional, but the person who reads it. Therefore, this book will not only help you better understand customer relationships. It will help you to understand better about you and your relationship with yourself, your close family and friends, the society you are in, and the world, the place where you live. And then, having understood all this better, you can make the choice to have a healthy relationship with your company's customers - or not - and that bears fruit - or not - leading you to a successful professional life and dignity - or not.

It will not be an easy journey, it's true. Because learning often means admitting mistakes, changing things we did not want. But this is relationship. And its beauty is the power to make us grow, evolve. However, one must be prepared for this. By allowing yourself the experience of reading this book, you will experience the relationship itself. Beyond Profit - Touching the invisible in customer relationships, is like a flight simulator: read it, absorb it, allow yourself to be impacted by the valuable knowledge passed on here by Leo, and you are ready to choose whether to relate your clients, your employees, your spouse, yourself, your Spirit...

JULIE ANNE CALDAS
JOURNALIST, OWNER OF THE TOPTEXT AND PROUDLY EDITOR OF THIS BOOK.

BEFORE WE START OUR JOURNEY

"**BEFORE** we start our journey into the unknown, I would like to invite you to turn this reading into an opportunity for dialogue.

If this material somehow catches your attention and you want to deepen your study and knowledge, I invite you to access my main pages on social networks or even directly through my email.

- **Blog at Exame.com** - http://exame.abril.com.br/blog/relacionamento-antes-do-marketing/ - que escrevo semanalmente juntamente com meu sócio Marcio Oliveira

- **Linked-in** - www.linkedin.com/in/lbarci/

- www.youdb.com.br – **youDb's** website, company I founded, with the aim of contributing to a better relationship between Companies and Clients

- www.facebook.com/youDb/ - **youDb's Facebook page**

I wish from now on a gratifying experience in your reading as it was for me to write this book.

Leonardo Barci
leonardo@barci.com.br

INTRODUCTION

"IF life is a school, then relationship is the university." I find this saying a bit true when it comes to relationships. Relationship means that in each interaction we will always have only part of the answer or the question. It is the opportunity we have that 1 + 1 is = 3, where "1" is inside a relationship. Mathematically impossible, it's true. But relationship is not something just rational.

Most of what I write down on paper from now on has been the practice and experience within my personal relationships and a day to day work. I found out that deepening on relationships is not for everyone or for every company. It is, in the first place, a choice. ***A conscious choice***.

After all, imagine that I told you that embarking on this journey the only guarantee is that you have no further guarantees. Would you still on board? Relationship is a portal. Just like painting, music, dance, martial arts and so many other human expressions, relationship is also a door to the divine.

Unlike the idea that some companies in the market are presenting, relationship is not something systematic, that can be organized step by step, packaged and then resold for everyone.

There is a very profound challenge when it comes to the relationship between company and client, which follows the same logic of human relations. Each person within the relationship is unique, different from the other(s). There are always similarities, but they cease as the relationship begins to deepen in truth. **Each of us is a universe, and the relationship is the expression of an initial division**. A division almost unconscious, if I may say so.

To understand marketing and the relationship between business and customers, we must also understand a little about human history. At the beginning.... Well, at the beginning there were no companies! Just as there were no customers.

Using our own planet as a reference, if we look at any contemporary tribe, that is, where social organization is still poorly structured and human relations and the environment are the basis, we will see that there is no great distance between people, or between them and their environment.

In a general way, history has evolved this way: the tribes grow and, with this growing, the first cities or structured societies begin to be formed. There comes a time when it is no longer possible for everyone to do everything. Someone dwells on the study and applications of the division of labor to be performed. This division leads to some form of exchange (negotiation) of products and services, which evolves into something more practical. Currency or money then comes up. Money brings the possibility of an even faster exchange. Someone in the middle of the path has the insight of creating a production line. Another discovers that systematizing things makes the production faster. And then we started with the so-called industrial era.

While all this is taking place, a figure that only far beyond will be recognized, is silently evolving, since the frantic search for growth leaves aside the importance of its counterpart. Yes, I'm talking about that figure that was almost forgotten during this whole story: **THE CLIENT!**

What few companies came to realize while looking at their own growth is that they only exist because someone bought their products or services. Company and customer are born at the same time. One does not exist without the other. Although all this has been a human creation, the two - company and client - are one, a pure consequence of each other.

That is the rational part of this whole story. There is, however, a subtler level that connects all. Some people call it a spiritual level. Others, transcendence. Still others call it a mystical level. But no matter what name you choose to give, the reality is that, things are linked in a way that is closer and deeper than we can perceive by looking only at the surface.

———————————| |———————————

WHAT FEW COMPANIES CAME TO REALIZE WHILE LOOKING AT THEIR OWN GROWTH IS THAT THEY ONLY EXIST BECAUSE SOMEONE PURCHASED THEIR PRODUCTS OR SERVICES. COMPANY AND CUSTOMER ARE BORN AT THE SAME TIME.

———————————| |———————————

Few years ago, this was only theory in Western society, but has recently become a "science case." The biologist and biochemist Rubert Sheldrack, to cite just one example, has gone deep into connections that go beyond what is perceptible. He calls these invisible connections by the name of: morphogenetic fields. I personally assume that relationships are more than we can observe now.

Do you need any proof? If we were to rely only on rational numbers and information, it would be quite difficult to justify why even knowing that more than a half of relationships and business are bound to end in no more than five years, we continue to marry and open businesses! The 'soled' idea in movies and in motivational talks that marriage is a great and eternal happiness and that a company is the way to freely independence is a fallacy. An illusion as great as the disconnection between humanity and the planet where we all live.

Based on this, the incessant search for understanding and reasoning every think is put in check. After all, what is the "reason" of starting up on a journey that you already know beforehand that you are more likely to fail than to succeed? At this point only something that is on a level beyond rational understanding would be able to explain why we continue to strive.

I try to say that the division between company and client follows the same principle of **the division between masculine and feminine. It naturally seeks for union**. A way to reconnect and reattach. It is a superior force that seeks to bring together separate parties. And I'm not looking for explanations here. At this moment, I'm just assuming that, it is the way it is.

Something that has become clear to me is that we are (paraphrasing The Little Prince) the relationships we cultivate. There is always the possibility of ending. In fact, this has been the first choice in most cases. And reality begins to get a bit more arid when we discover that we have changed relationships, but the problems remain the same. It's the so-called "reality check." And to transform reality, one must first know it, so that it can be transposed. Only by bringing the unknown to ourselves and in our companies, we can discover solution.

1 – WHAT IS A RELANTIONSHIP?

LIFE is relationship! To understand what that means, you must **live** relationships. I've heard a lot of stories about the difference between knowledge and wisdom. Some even quite elaborate and deepen the two meaning. In a simple way, I see knowledge as something that comes exclusively from the outside, someone transmits something to you and you "learn". You can believe without questioning - but it only lasts until your belief is tested for the first time and you begin to question whether what you have learned was true - or you can test yourself that knowledge and have a direct experience of it. What follows experience is what I would point out as wisdom. ***Experience brings you the opportunity, but wisdom comes from an inner experience in which you "just know", without the need of any proof***.

I see relationships on this way. I can write pages and pages of theoretical content on how it starts, how to evolve it and how to end it if the things come "too heavy." But in the end, it will only be borrowed knowledge. If you don't want to experiment or don't have a basic "repertoire" of relationships already established, my words will end up being of no meaning for you.

And to have that experience is easy. Is just a matter of choice. And experiencing it, in a broad sense. Because, as I said at the beginning of this chapter, **life is relationship**. It means that the way we behave in every situation, shows the degree of our relationships with other people and even with the things involved. It seems exaggerated? Let's take a simple example:

> "Someone leaves in a town on the top of a mountain and decided to go to the nearest beach. There, the person puts on his parasol, enjoys the sunny day and has lunch in the local tent. When the person departs, he leaves the garbage in the sand and return to its house on the top of the mountain."

Of course, what immediately impresses in this history is that the person had left the garbage on the beach. And maybe that's even important; Or maybe not.... We are already going to be more objective at this situation. But first let's look at the whole picture.

If this person has gone to the beach alone but is married and has children, it may show that the relationship at home is not so good, that he needs some time alone, or that the person does not care much about the people around him. If the person has a good relationship with his neighbors on the mountain, he may have been accompanied by them, which shows that the person has an established relationship with the people in his area. Either way, going alone or with someone else is already a sign of the type and depth of relationships the person has established and is experiencing at that moment. Finally, let's go to the trash! We could say that he is not likely to see the beach as part of his own home - after all, it is unusual for someone to throw garbage on the floor of their own house. In this case, we conclude that it also has a relationship with the coastal region: negative.

> **(Taking this example, it is worth taking the time to say that if we look at the effects of climate change, we will begin to notice that, as humanity, we have not had a good relationship with our own planet.)**

What I'm calling your attention to is that each attitude and each "non-attitude" shows the relationship we have with people or things, near or distant. And I'm not saying that we need to have a deep relationship with everything and everyone. The scale is quite wide. It's natural for you to have a greater openness to the people in your home than to the janitor. **You may have good relationships with everyone, but at different levels of depth**. In fact, the depth of a relationship is a door of true union. The deeper you go, the greater the need to open yourself to the other - and the greater his or her fragility will be.

These principles I have exposed applied equally to business to consumer relations. Not all customers want to relate on the same level.

Some want to go into the store, buy what they need and interact as little as possible. But others want to be recognized as a regular customer and still get some branded stuff at home. And there, it remains for the company to choose whether to open to that depth.

A company that chooses to "love" its customers, i.e. being open to listening and offering the best it can, despite the difficulties, is on a higher scale as to the depth of the relationship. That is, the company is willing to take risks, but still do its best.

Here is a commentary on general legislation: it says that all clients should have the same benefits and equal treatment. I am a fan of democracy, but this point in the law ends up distorting the freedom of relationship a little, for to establish equality, in this case, would be to curtail the will. In contrast, I think that millage programs, when well applied, have been a great tool to differentiate clients according to their desires and attitudes.

Ultimately, relationship is exposure. The companies I see as having the best relationship with their clients are not the ones that show up the most on television or those who straggle least. But those who are open to admit their mistakes and improve daily, with the aim of always seeking to be better for the "other half of the relationship": **THE CLIENT**.

I have recently saw the case of a world-class coffee shop that has been found to transfer its customers' data in unsafe databases. From the point of view of technology, this is a delicate and even reprehensible attitude. I decided to be attentive to what would happen next, and the repercussion from the part of the customers was minimal. Reading a little more about the history of the company in this regard, I discovered that there had been a recent turn around in the business and that many things had been changed. The focus had been on coffee quality and on customer service. The rest ended up being a consequence of this decision. The company's billing and technology systems were changed, which were quite outdated. Along the way, the company, at the request of customers, decided to implement an innovative system of recognition in stores and to make the wi-fi service available to all its customers. All this attention with them, in my opinion, has taken the issue of data security to a lower level. That is: although somehow the customer may have felt insecure in the process, they realized that the company was sincerely doing its best to serve them.

This brings us to two key points for the definition of this chapter. The first of these is that although the company may seek to do its best, a relationship **ALWAYS** involves two parties. Therefore, if the customer does not want, no matter how much the company has an interest on it, there will be no deep relationship. **It is a choice of two sides**. The second key point, which for me is vital, is that the company, if it chooses to have good relationships, needs to be open to admitting its own mistakes and, above all, being an agent of change itself. Does it seem like a difficult advice to follow? Not if we look at it based on the knowledge each of us has of our own personal relationships. One of the relations, in my opinion, that most closely matches what happens between a company and its customers is the relationship of two persons.

If we look at the core of this type of relationship, we usually have three forces that build it: eroticism, sex, and love. Each one with its function. To explain them in a simple way, I would say: eroticism generates approximation, sex generates pleasure and fruits (or children, if you prefer) and love supports the relationship. The words are a bit "hot," but not at all distant from a person to person relationship, are they?

So, between the company and customer, there are characteristics that correspond to these three, with similar functions, and which are also fundamental to sustain the main pillar of this relationship, which involves making business, but invariably also emotion. Connecting with your client, therefore, means making the decision to embark on an unexpected, challenging journey, but which, if experienced in a pleasant way for both sides, can be as rewarding and valiant as a marriage that, despite the discussions, lasted "until death separated them".

2 - WHY RELATE?

AT this point you are probably wondering if it is worthwhile to establish any kind of conscious relationship. After all, if we "let the currents of life carry us" will end up bringing the problems in front of us, so... why go after them anyway? But that's not how it works, because relationships are also bridges to get where we want. More than that: they take us to what we need. "It is impossible to be happy alone," would endorse a Brazilian poet.

What not only poets would say is that each of us, whether as a person or as a company, has within us two main latent desires. The desire for happiness, or self-realization, and the desire to serve or reciprocate others in some way. And the bigger the first, the more natural the latter. How and why things are like this, I honestly cannot say; I just feel, I perceive them looking around. I could even go through a few chapters of the book elaborating and rambling on what would be a possible explanation. But it is easier to say only that, in my point of view, what drives us to have these two desires is something that is intrinsic to anyone: love.

Yes love. Perhaps a strange word for a book intended to uncover the challenges in the relationships between companies and their customers. However, it is a fact that business people who have dealt with this theme, had also called attention to them, whether it has been the intention or not. The explanation: without a real attention and dedication for what we do, that goes beyond the limits of rationality, we can hardly get anywhere. Without a connection with what is essential in us and in our corporations, our daily work becomes empty and meaningless. ***The attitude of doing something just to make money is starting to look valueless and fragile. Joy comes to be in making the other happy***. And in the case of the company, the other is the customer. And to have it dealt with in the best way is, in my understanding, true service.

_____||_____

EACH OF US, EITHER AS A PERSON OR AS A COMPANY, HAS WITHIN TWO MAJOR LATENT DESIRES. THE DESIRE FOR HAPPINESS, OR SELF-REALIZATION, AND THE DESIRE TO SERVE OR RECIPROCATE TO OTHERS IN SOME WAY.

_____||_____

The basis for this definition, whether a company is focused on its client or not, is what the American author Simon Sinek calls "the Why of the organizations." The old 'business mission' nowadays needs more to have a look on purpose than just being a catch phrase. This "Why" is what allows the true connection between business and customer. And, as we have already said, one does not exist without the other.

A few years ago, I opened a new business that has since made me go through a profound personal change. My main desire at that time when opening the company was self-expression. I was a little tired of working inside companies and wanting to do things differently, but I ended up running into some sort of limitation on the organization or the clients. However, as I started my own company, I soon discovered that the limitations were not "outside" but in myself. It was the first step on the path of fulfilling my own desires: the search for happiness.

Even at the beginning, I bumped into a cross road. One that may seem a paradox at that moment: in the moment of my decision to start a new business, I did not consider that I would have to relate to a growing number of people and companies. But in the end, what each of these relationships was bringing to me was simply understanding myself. Therefore, because I have passed through this experience and acquired such wisdom (more than knowledge, remember), I can affirm that there is no other answer to the title question of this chapter other than this one: **It is impossible to reach the Why of your company, to accomplish whatever it is you intend to do, without having some degree of relationship with your customers. The relationship is - fortunately - inevitable.**

3 - WHAT IS NEEDED?

IT SEEMS obvious, but answering in a simple way, I would say that for any kind of relationship it involves at least two parties. And not only that: it is also necessary that both choose to be part of the relationship. ***A conscious choice***.

If we established a scale from one to ten for this consciousness, we would have: starting on one, that kind of relationship in which there may be no awareness of one or both that something connects them; And in ten, the full awareness of both sides that both are responsible for everything that happens within the relationship.

The problem encountered at the beginning of the scale is that it establishes that type of relationship in which there is some form of exploitation. In it, a part (or both, eventually) asks, "what is in it for me here?". It is the reason why of the explorers. Nothing against those pioneers who search for new horizons for human life, those who found frontiers before them and decide to go ahead. I'm talking about that kind of explorer who just pulls out and with nothing contributes to the whole. On the other hand, at the top of the scale, we have relationships that emerge from a conscious choice and the consequence is that the two sides begin to realize the impact they generate on each other.

I have a deep love and respect for Brazil. I was born in this wonderful land. I am a son and grandson of immigrants, people who have chosen to live and bequeath their generations here. But looking at the current social stage of our country, I see that in many places and in many ways, we are still between one and two on this scale of conscious relationship. Using our own environment as a learning tools, we have only recently begun to realize that we are responsible for the political and social situation in our own country. The politicians and social managers did not happen to occupy their positions by chance. Although with a monarchy at the beginning, a military coup in the middle and some of the clashes along the way, today we are, in fact, a democracy.

Our ancestors that already lived here knew that: ***freedom sometimes needs to be reconquered***. While the people of Africa and elsewhere were enslaved and brought here, the Indians understood that servitude is also a kind of relationship from which one can choose to participate. Many of them naturally died to prove their point of view, but with that, our ancestors had to reflect on whether this was a healthy relationship.

On the other side of the scale, I see companies that have been growing at impressive rates inviting their customers to be part of their strategies. Companies such as Amazon.com, which includes their customers as a direct and objective part of the relationship. It's a win-win model. The more exchange there is between the company and its customers, the more everyone - and in this case "everyone" is quite a crowd! - wins. The Amazon's customer, receives better indications of products and services; suppliers more accurate information about their production and inventory management and better exposure; the company greater satisfaction in being able to deliver what it really wants to, besides having greater profitability and assertiveness in its strategies.

The good news is that, like almost everything in this life, it is always time to start changing. Even my perception up to this point in that life has been this: **For there to be a relationship, it is necessary that over time there will be an evolution in the scale**. People may begin with little awareness of why they are relating, but over time it is necessary for that consciousness to expand and become a conscious choice.

In short, you can do everything as an entrepreneur or marketer - and the same goes for personal relationships - to do your best for a good relationship with your customers, to be attentive in the details in the "game of seduction"; But there will be a point where the customer will also have to choose whether to be part of the relationship or not.

Relationship is a dance that cannot be danced alone. And the more committed the dancers are in making this joint dance work, the more beautifully the choreography will be performed.

4 - HOW A RELANTIONSHIP BEGINS

IN THE first chapter, we talked about comparing business-customer relationship with the relationship of a couple. And if, among a couple, eroticism plays the role of bringing the two parties together, seeking words more appropriate to the business world, I would say that the beginning of the relationship starts with seduction. And seduction, from the companies' side, means, to show up, "to sell yourself" and, with that, attract the attention of possible future clients. Advertising, for example, performs this function with mastery.

Seduction has and will always play a key role in generating that initial spark, that first movement of the client toward the company for the relationship to begin. As a couple, eroticism bridges sex and love; from a business point of view, seduction, or publicity, bridges the first purchase and the continuity of the relationship. Excessive publicity (or seduction), however, exhausts itself. It's like a platonic love that never comes true. It is an ideal relationship that never happens in real life. And, citing the gap between what the company talks about and what it really does, it's where the confusion begins. Because fantasy (or eroticism) is not reality, and to live as if it is, is a certain path to disappointment.

Anyone who has been hooked at least once by the webs of seduction, knows that the woman he loves will not be in that short, low-cut dress every day, or the man in that first-class suit and beard. Daily, the relationship offers its 'reality', its challenges. Seduction (eroticism) is sometimes confused with a continued relationship (love), after all the relationship is happening. And the consequence for businesses is that it begins to believe that it's the promotions that sustain the relationship with it's customers. If that's your model, beware! Want to test it? Stop promoting and see which customers continues to buy. These, and only these, are those who want a relationship in truth. The rest only seek the cheapest option.

Just being seductive does not create sustainable relationships. Seduction is variable, as is promotion. It generates waves of new customers, who, the same way they come, they also go. It demands from companies something unreal: to be a new and attractive company every day. And I am not talking here about the laudable act of innovating, but about going out making changes that do not create anything perennial. It's as if every morning we wake up with someone different at our side, who has decided to change, whether physically or emotionally - sometimes it can be good, but happening every day, is likely to generate relative discomfort and as a consequence, break out the relationship.

Companies that only seduce new customers show that deep down they do not want any kind of commitment. They're companies that have some fear of relating more deeply. It is as if the next customer is always better than the old ones. It is saying that what the company already has at home is not good enough to be worthy of receiving an excellent product or service. Therefore, seduce; but always keeping in mind the next step.

Seduction held, it's time to go to the next step: the first purchase! For me, this is an important moment because it is when the customer entrusts what he has of greater value to the company. I'm not just talking about money here (yes, it's important too), but mostly about the choice. Customer's choice. With the purchase, he says, through a concrete action: "I chose your store, your brand to start a relationship". As much as the customer may leave tomorrow, at this moment, for this purchase, he chooses only you! And here it is what I call creative force injection: the company starts to have energy (trust), deposited by their customers, people to whom it can effectively deliver its products and services; And ultimately earns money to follow up with their needs.

Skillful companies are those who know how to take advantage of their seduction skills and generate business and make it a lasting relationship. On the other hand, a company that loses its capacity for seduction ages as a brand; customers find out that nothing changes. Good customers will always respect and admire the company, but they will realize that she (the company) is no longer interested in evolving.

_____||_____

COMPANIES THAT JUST SEDUCE NEW CUSTOMERS SHOW THAT DEEP DOWN, THEY DO NOT WANT ANY KIND OF COMMITMENT.

_____||_____

In the same way, the client also has its power of seduction and fulfillment. He transforms, changes his channels of relationship, matures as a person, requires more and, buy! Seduction, for the customer, is also a search for the unknown: "what will the company that I admire is doing right now? "; "Do they have something new? "; "I love that product / service that only they know how to do"; "I like the attention they give me so much...". In response, the company needs to be attentive to its customers: "Will my products / services be as well accepted as I think they are? "; "Do my customers continue to buy in the same way and for the same purpose? "; "Are their needs still the same? ".

As part of this process, it's important never to think that you know everything about your customers. A survey always reveals partially who they are, as well as the information in the database. But the customer's life is much more than that. Their purchase relationship, for example, will never be exclusive; They will continue to relate to other companies. Maybe they even try to be faithful to the same product or service, but most of the time not even that. And what happens to this network of possibilities is that the customer will always have a basis of comparison about what a good relationship is.

Another point to be taken: the relationship that works is one in which there is involvement from both sides, and that is why excessive seduction is dangerous. It creates laziness and accommodation from the side of the client. The company does everything and consequently the customer does nothing (or do very little). Therefore, **in an ideal relationship, seduction, fulfillment (purchase) and desire for continuity and renewal are always present in a balanced way**.

To close this chapter, I end with a practical example of what can be a good approximation or seduction and what would be the opposite of that.

Imagine for a moment the following hypothetical scene: a customer walks into a shop and approaches the salesperson, and then a dialogue begins...

CLIENT: Hi, good morning!

COMPANY (attendant): Good morning.

CLIENT: I just saw your store outside and I think that you have the profile of what I'm offering.

COMPANY: OK...

CLIENT: What can I do for you?

COMPANY: Well... My main goal is to sell more, so I think you can help me. I would like you to buy as many products as possible from my store. Preferably those which have higher profit margins. If possible dividing in plots, thus, in addition to the value of the sale, I can also earn some interest.

CLIENT: It seems a little strange to me, a little bit one sided... But okay, I got my paycheck this week and I have spare money. I think I can help you. Anything else?

COMPANY: Yes, could you leave me your personal information? It's just that I want you to be loyal to my brand and buy only from me, even if it is more advantageous for you to buy from the store next door. And I also want to send you communications, preferably on the cheapest channel. Then, whatever stimulus you get, go back to my store and buy again as much as possible. That way I'll be happy!

CLIENT: Well, now it's really weird, because it seems like you're not interested in what's important to me or what will make difference in my life. But okay, I was the one who started this conversation, coming into your store and asking what you wanted.

COMPANY: Okay, I will think about what you said. But I still think selling more is the most important thing to me.

This dialogue, although somewhat strange, unfortunately reflects the reality of many of the relationships between companies and clients. And the point of view of the relationship should not be "what I can get out of this relationship," but rather "what I have to offer." Could it be that if we changed the desire to Sell More for Better Selling, would not the dialogue naturally happen in a different way? Maybe even with the customer start saying...

CLIENT: Hi, good morning! Your store attracted me for some reason. It looks like an empty shed all painted white, but at the same time there is something here that catches me.

COMPANY: Hi, good morning! Yes, for the time being, what you said is true. Until I know a little more about you and what you need, I do not have much to offer. So, let's start with some direction... I, for example, like technology, I have some ability with that. Maybe from this we can find a way that joins you and me. Before I offer you any product or service, tell me a little bit about yourself. To start, your name, please. It will make it easier to talk to you personally. And then, you can tell me a little bit about your day to day life...

CLIENT: Hum, I like it, you look nice to me. My name is Carlos, I'm married, I have two young children, a seven-year-old boy and a five-year-old girl. I work far from where I live and my biggest challenge is being able to talk to my wife during my work time. She works in a part-time job away from our home, and the other half of the day she stays at home with our kids.

COMPANY: Thank you Carlos for sharing a little bit of you and your day to day life. Now look around you and see if anything catches your eye.

CUSTOMER: Wow! What magic is this? Where did these products come from? There are small appliances and bigger ones. What are they?

COMPANY: These are the latest generation of mobile phones. Did not I tell you I was good with technology? Did any of them catch your attention?

CLIENT: These minors.
COMPANY: Hum, I see you have a good eye. I'll take the liberty of suggesting something. Can I?

CLIENT: Yes, of course! Apparently, you know exactly what I'm looking for...

COMPANY: OK, I'll suggest you a package of product and services. This device that caught your attention seems to meet what you need to improve your day to day life. It's a small cell phone with a two-day battery, that means you can be with it all day long, make calls to your wife and still come home at night with some charge. Yes, I know, you will say, that there is no phone at home yet. Am I correct?

CLIENT: Almost. My wife has a prepaid cell phone, but whenever we need to talk, the phone is out of credit.

COMPANY: I have two suggestions, Carlos: one is you can subscribe a postpaid mobile phone, but this may be more than you need now, after all, I understood that during the day there will be more occasional conversations with your spouse. The second suggestion, which seems to me the best for you now, is a home line that has a lower entry and monthly cost. With this, I add a service to you of lower cost calls between your cell phone and your home. I can still... Well, I think I'm talking too much already. First tell me, does this help you?

CUSTOMER: Damn, I see that with the few information I gave you, you really know what I need. Oops! What is this screen showing cartoons that appeared here next to me?

COMPANY: Ah, this! Excuse me, I cannot control myself... This is a cable-TV service. Since you said you have two small children, I thought you might be interested. It's a basic package, but it does have some cartoons included in the package. We are working on some new features so you can control the schedule and programs that will be available to your children. After all, I imagine you would not want them to watch TV all the time, but maybe it can help your wife when she's at home and need to prepare something for them to eat, or even a break.

CLIENT: Wow, you're already seducing me, are not you?

COMPANY: (Laughter). Yes, but the truth is, as I told you, I love technology and I'm good with it. So, if I can offer you anything else within what I like to do, it will be a privilege for me.

CLIENT: Okay, for now I'll keep your first offer. In line with your day-to-day care, we can evolve our relationship.

> *(Yes, as much as we are still in the seduction phase, a long-term relationship can be built from the beginning, which is where we include Selling at long term, which will be discussed later.)*

COMPANY: That's right, I'm at your disposal. I would like to have the opportunity to serve you in the future. Would you mind leaving your personal information? I'm sending you communications, and when it's convenient, you come back here to do business. Would you mind leaving your contact information?

CLIENT: Sure, with great pleasure!

And finish. Phase of seduction completed successfully!

5 - THE CHOICE TO GO AHEAD

THIS is a challenging moment in the relationship. Challenging both for the company and - or perhaps even more so - for the customer. A proof of this is that some marketers treat this moment as a point of "cognitive dissonance". The explanation of this expression means that when "one part" of the customer decides something and "another part" does not have the same certainty - or really disagrees.

This is especially true for higher-value purchases, where the relationship will inevitably follow for several months, such as buying a car, a home, or even a new mobile subscription. Generally, the heart part says: "right decision! New car in the garage "; While the other part (the pocket) says: "Did I made the right choice? It will be another 59 months to pay out this car... ". Some companies, knowing this, even formally include positive reinforcement in salespeople training, by including phrases such as "Congratulations on your purchase, you made the right choice! ".

Going back to our comparison with the relation of two, I think maybe, because of the difficulty in compromising, terms like "stay for a night" have become popular. Dating is the first concrete step of compromise between different parties. And if from those who made the request is a step to happiness, whoever accepts the invite must be at the same 'page', or will think long before answering. Similarly, for the company making a long-term sale is excellent, but for the customer, depending on how it feels, can be a challenging time.

I know there are other reasons, but for me the volume of disposable cell phones that flooded the market is the reflection of not making a commitment to a continuous relationship between company and customer. Doing the math, depending on the case, a postpaid mobile comes out cheaper than a prepaid. But who wants to date when they know they will not even be able to call their loved one if they decide to end their relationship? We need to understand that this is the moment to transcend, to leave the common place and establish a first commitment.

To avoid any kind of misinterpretation, I sought the meaning of **TRANSCEND** before using the word. According to the dictionary, it means: "be or go beyond the range or limits of...". To reinforce the idea that I want to show you, I choose the term **GO BEYOND**. Yes, it is challenging. Dating seems easy but not everyone wants to give up being able to have all the other options to date "just one".

And as I said, the challenge of this decision is mainly from the customer, the company has very little influence on it. However, I believe that it is important to dedicate a chapter to this phase of the relationship, so that you, as a company, can understand in more details what is going on in the head, heart and pocket of your wooer, the client.

If well resolved, this phase of dating happens smoothly. It's almost an eternal learning about the company and the customer. Every day a new discovery, in a positive way! You are "getting to know each other". And if the answer "yes" was given in a conscious way, it is at this stage that coincidences happens that neither the company nor the client had foreseen. That's when the unexpected begins to emerge. But, in my point of view, this transcendent connection only happens when the two sides (company and its customer) begin to express their essence, that is, each one gives its best.

If we were talking about a cafeteria, it is that moment when the coffee is so yummy and well prepared that the venue happens to be a reference in the city. Not for lack of other options, but because that is perceived as the best cafe in town. That's when the customer walks a few more blocks to go there, it's when he feels good paying for a simple coffee and, whether it's spending $ 10 or $ 15, he thinks his money is being well spent. It is when the customer's time spent in the cafeteria can be used to produce new projects. He starts thinking about his own customers - yes, this positive wheel turns from company to customer, from customer (like a professional who works at some other company) to his customers, and so on. And that's where the unexpected happens: the relationship **transcends** itself.

This scenario, however, only works when company and client are on the same level of awareness within the relationship. The company understands its impact on society, and the customer understands the impact of buying (or not) from that company. Even when there is a gap, the effort on one side must be greater to reach equilibrium. For example, in the case of foreign brands that land in the country from places with a higher socio-cultural level: the company must also be aware that it must educate the market in some way. This is what has been happening in recent years with initiatives in the financial market that support financial education actions for the "new unbanked". This means that the side with greater awareness knows the impact that the company's market entry can cause, and starts to contribute to the development of the other.

And do not think that this is just the role of foreign companies, from more developed countries. Talk to some Brazilian company that has landed in so-called developed world markets and you will see how much learning it has had to develop in their clients and how they have also learned from this movement. Whether it be legislation, entry barriers or even the relationship with a new public with a higher cultural level and formal education. Dating is a phase of much learning about yourself, in which both the company and the clients develop, each one within their reality. But for this it is vital to expose yourself to the relationship, to accept that, yes, there may be flaws and points of improvement on both sides.

If a company has never had delivery problems, it is certain that it never took their products beyond the entry door. An excess of problems in this area, however, may indicate that the company must improve its attention in the delivery systems. The customer, at that moment, becomes an excellent indicator of improvements for the company. So, the first step is to accept that flaws exist and will become apparent the moment the company and customers decide to have a more conscious relationship. On the customer side, it is time to demand a better-quality service. If he understands that his attention (or cash) is not being matched by the company, he will question that. He will want more.

And what happens if neither companies nor clients are aware of the relationship, do not want to expose themselves, see failures and are not willing to change? Well, in that case it is quite likely that formal ways will emerge to try to put order in the house, such as laws. That is, in one way or another - either by will or by pressure from outside - there will be a sign that something is not going well.

Yes, relationship takes time and needs hard work. But we must not avoid this path. Friction is part of the relationship. Things will go wrong, but that does not mean that in the end it's not worth it. Because error makes us grow, improve us, get us on the right path. And, if you've ever had something similar in your relationship as a couple, why not try with your company?

Believe: Companies that start being well seen by their customers are not the ones with least problems. I'd say the opposite. The difference is in awareness and work for a better relationship with your various audiences. And let the customer do not deluded himself: if he really believes in the phrase "this company is a necessary evil," then he himself is part of the problem.

And how then do you reach that level of consciousness, **transcend** the relationship and transform a simple "dating" into the "first real step"? Considering that the company is usually the one with the highest level of knowledge and preparation **about its own products and services**, let's start with it - but without forgetting that the responsibility is mutual. Company, here are some advices:

❯ Listen to your customer. Really! Bring it close to you. Not to minimize complaints but as a way to evolve the relationship.

❯ Seek bringing light to small problems, be it communication, delivery, production, training, etc. I would say that here lies the key to much success.

❯ Look for the more open and transparent communication possible. Telling the truth, even if it is difficult, works better than trying to cover it up...

❯ Seek ways of reducing the gap between what you say you do and what you actually do – Try the Walk the Talk path. Do not be shy to admit that you may be lying! Even without knowing. Recognizing your current stage brings more mutual awareness and improves the relationship.

❯ Do not be afraid of intimacy. When people want to approach your company, look for ways to do it. And here's a personal case: I worked for nine of the biggest automakers in Brazil. In every case, I could see the desire that the customers had to know the respective factories of their cars and be close to where things really happened. Just like in a personal relationship, you probably would not want to visit your room (or the place of new product development), but perhaps knowing the kitchen and the living room (the factory) already give it a sense of belonging and satisfaction. In summary, the message here is: let the customer be part of.

❯ And, finally, be open to something unexpected that might come along the way. This is how companies reinvent themselves...

6 - WHY DOES NOT WORK?

LIFE always strives for balance. I remember an old commercial with Chico Anysio (a famous Brazilian actor), I think one of the few he did, for a brand of VCR - well, if you're under 25, I'd suggest searching the internet about what a video cassette is. It was a very sensitive commercial, comparing life to a video recording. The text went something like this: "Imagine that you had complete control over your life and your history. Imagine that through a remote control you could go back in time and relive the good times. Spend these moments in slow motion to get the most out of it. Skip the parts that do not interest you. Forward in high speed the unpleasant moments. Pause and eternalize an orgasm." And then the commercial ended with Chico presenting the brand's VCR and saying that all that was possible using it. It was an intense text, but at the same time simply true. ***It's what we all want: more pleasure and happiness, less pain and discomfort***.

As soon as the phase of the courtship between the company and the client passes, the complaints and the annoyances begin. As much as the company wanted new customers, there are lamentations such as "the customer did not understand what we are offering"; "The product is being consumed in the wrong way"; "The customer does not pay up-to-date, we'll send his name to the credit protection service." On the part of the client, the scenario is not very different: "this company promised the world and poorly delivery the minimum"; "I've been waiting for a response to my complaint for several days and they do not even send a smoke sign"; "I will denounce this company to law, or rather, I will spread it on social networks how bad they are".

I do not question the truth on both sides, but remember: Dating is over! And this is the "**tough reality**." If we think of a personal relationship, incredible as it may seem, dating can last longer than dating itself. It sometimes ends very close to the wedding. Sometimes later. Sometimes many years later. Dating is, in part, an illusion. It is rare for someone to make a derogatory comment at this stage. Everything is going well, and the devotion is such that people are even capable of killing if their partner is threatened in some way - the so-called passion crimes.

I am not saying that the courtship or the end of it is something "right" or "wrong," only that, inevitably, one's projection on the other will fall, and reality will sooner or later have to be faced. And, well, at this point it is becoming clear why companies so desperately want new customers... Because dating is really a delight. Maybe the best phase of life.

So much so that many people choose to end a courtship by beginning another, suffering only momentarily for the end, but knowing that a new passion heals everything. That is why, at this point, you need to decide: you can choose to stop, just like many companies that just stay in the dating phase, or go ahead and find out what comes after that phase. Having said that, I begin to uncover a little of what, at least in my experience, has been a very realistic path to solution. I call this path of **reciprocity**.

Some personal willingness is needed to open up and see that behind every relationship there is an invisible dynamic. Something that connects us like people and companies before we even meet. Such dynamics may be, for example, the customer's need to buy a new product or service, or the (if unconscious) need of the company to find a "problem customer" ahead, which will give some sign that some things need to be improved.

Imagine that you are a customer of a mobile company. Stop paying the service for three months and you will discover something: in the fourth month, maybe in the fifth, you will stop being a "person" and become a **defaulting customer**. Of course, you will still be a person, but also a defaulting customer. You have learned a new thing about yourself. And who told you this was the company, from the relationship that both established.

Reciprocity is the force that unites opposites. I can say with some confidence that these encounters that rarely generate any sort of relationship happen by chance. Whether this is conscious or not. If you have or have ever had a stable personal relationship, you know what I'm talking about. It is necessary to be aware that the relationship will have the door open for the discovery of several points of improvement, **on both sides**. And although I talk a lot about the company's side, I would also like to point out the **responsibility of clients and consumers**. For this, I will quickly tell you a personal story.

I have at home a water filter system that is rented. From time to time, the company comes to my residence to do periodic maintenance. Usually they make an active contact to suggest this schedule, but the last time I had to make the call to ask for it. In fact, some calls... Two or three attempts to visit my home and some difficulties later, the review was made.

I was a little annoyed and started a search for another brand. I came to evaluate the purchase of a new filter. But the irritation passed away, and I kept the service. Sometime later, there was a problem in the filter and it was no longer turning off the water flow. I was angry, but realized at that moment that **the company had the same weight in the relationship than I do**. Yes, I could have canceled the service months before. After all, I am the customer! And this second time, I was even more dissatisfied, because it was four or five days without water to drink. But this has generated for me the opportunity to learn **reciprocity**: the service of the company is relevant to me and I could have canceled; But, yes, they can also somehow "cancel" the service when they no longer want the customer.

And this is not something new, companies have always had the ability to "fire their customers". Incidentally, in the past, I think they did it even cleaner by the way. An example: several years ago, Bank Boston (which in 2006 was bought by Itau Bank, lost its name here in Brazil), in a controversial act of sincerity, sent a letter to some of the clients of its database disconnecting them from the Bank, in sum, they did not have the right profile to be Bank Boston's clients. The attitude provoked revolt at the time, on accusations of prejudice - and we will not even have the merit of judging it here. The fact is that today this continues to happen, companies continue to "choose" customers, or choosing which customers they do not want. And they do this not with an honest letter, but by offering poor services, causing problems. Until they leave. And feel possibly guilty about it.

When I realized that I had been the poor customer, this reflection showed me that although we still have a paternalistic bias in consumer legislation in Brazil - perhaps a lot because of the systematic exploitation of people's lack of knowledge - the relationship needs to be **balanced**. There must be **mutual respect**. No, I'm not being innocent and denying that many companies do not need to improve their practices. But I want to point out that the customer is also **responsible for the quality of this relationship**. I see, in the end, that there needs to be openness on both sides for the **"YES"** to a better relationship.

I am speaking here of something quite subtle. We are evolving in Brazil to put our demands into action. We are changing the level of consumption and citizenship, **failing to complain that the problem is in some external entity and assuming part of the responsibility**. And denying this fact is denying the energy it contains.

_____| |_____

COMPANIES CONTINUE TO "CHOOSE" THE CUSTOMERS, AND DO THIS NOT WITH AN HONEST, CAREFUL LETTER, BUT BY OFFERING POOR SERVICES, CAUSING PROBLEMS.

_____| |_____

In the case I mentioned above, I learned that the problem that happened to me was a manufacturing defect of the product that the company had been aware of for at least seven years. I say this because this same problem happened in a friend's company, and the technician who came to my house to do the repair confirmed that the company was performing the change of the trigger button, ***however, only when the customer complains***. Well, both in my case and in my friend's case, it was hours of water leakage at the maximum capacity of the filter, which, by my estimate, should mean about 500 liters of water. Yes, the company is hurting its customers. The question is, is the company aware of this?

With so much difficulty and so many challenges, I imagine that you, the reader, are asking yourself: is there a true relationship that is good for everyone? And if it exists, the next question is: how to get to it? The answer to the first question is: yes. For the second one, it may not be very pleasant: the only effective step I've known so far is to **give up control and security**. From the control that the company can predict and influence customer reactions and the assurance that the company is always doing the best and can avoid any kind of problem. The best way is to give up the idea that company and the customer do not do any harm to each other with their actions.

Until these steps are taken, we will have a fanciful, superficial relationship. But do not be discouraged! According to some authors, we are in the age of truth in relationships. So, embrace the truth in your company's relationship with your customers and take advantage, therefore, it is from this openness that comes the real freedom.

7 - HOW TO "FIX" IT

WHETHER consciously or not, we are co-creators of our destiny. Be it as a person or as a company. ***Every effect has its own cause***. And the responsibility for the business world that we live in is of everyone: clients, companies (and entrepreneurs), government and society. Working with relationship consulting I had the opportunity to see in practice what I suspected for a while: Clients attracted by promotion just want one thing - promotion. Cause and effect!

At the beginning of a project in a client of ours, the person in charge of conducting the work, told us that the company literally had a coupon room from the last promotion. As a good direct marketing professional, I told her that it was a great opportunity to increase the number of people in their database. The manager simple told us:

- Well, look, last year's promotion we followed that idea. Of the millions of coupons, we received, we took a sample of about 100,000 and sent them for typing. And we found that less than 1% of these people figure in our database.

So far, it seemed like a great opportunity to take advantage of the 99% of the remaining names. But she continued:

- We started a relationship strategy with these people without much success. And we ended up finding out that what they really wanted was a short, very short, promotion-like relationship!

When it comes to relationships, there are two fundamental principles that make "the wheel spin". For those who are married or have a stable relationship with another person, perhaps the following is easy to understand. **These are the principles of activation and acceptance**. Or male and female principle. Or reason and emotion. **One does not exist without the other**. And nature is proof of this...

In a nutshell, I would say that activation is action itself. And it's so real these days that we're talking about "customer activation." It's practically acting in the name of the client without letting him take any "re-action". Your counterpart? **Acceptance**, the inner movement of letting things happen. Anyone who has worked in the field knows exactly what the "faith" means regarding sprouting from a seed.

In business, **creation is the union of these two things - activation and acceptance, or masculine and feminine**. Again, reason and emotion. The balance between the two is (as well as in nature) fundamental. Too much activation causes dependence! Too much acceptance causes paralysis - or even laziness!

Looking at the relationships between company and customers, I see an overactivity in most relationships. Promotion-type is the extreme principle of activation. It is doing the possible (and sometimes even the impossible, selling below cost) for the customer to buy something - "let the wheel spin a little and then we go". The problem is you cannot do this all the time. Want to see a proof of it?

Imagine one of the largest search portals in the world (well, I guess we do not need to talk about names, do we?). I do not know their history deeply, but I know there was some activation in the beginning - putting a server on line, developing a search algorithm, fetching pages and forming an initial index, making a page available, inviting people and then... wait... From there the activity becomes much more maintenance and waiting than action. Even because changing the algorithm or the home initial page too much, makes it difficult for users to understand and continue use it.

So, from that point of waiting, people had to take an action: the action of typing www.search_engine_number_one.com. Many, thousands of times. Until that became big enough so the search engine was already set up as the home page for several devices, people had to take the action of putting it as their homepage or typing their address with each new search.

_____||_____

THE EQUILIBRIUM BETWEEN THE TWO IS (AS WELL AS IN NATURE) FUNDAMENTAL. OVERALL ACTIVATION CAUSES DEPENDENCE! TOO MUCH ACCEPTANCE CAUSES PARALYSIS - OR EVEN LAZINESS!

_____||_____

And, from there, it seems tempting that we do the part of the client and leave everything configured so he does not even need to remember the search engine brand. Well, in the short term, it may even be the best option for current customers. But think about your children. If they never need to enter the address, it is possible that at some point www.search_engine_number_TWO.com begins to work on brand awareness, and it is a question of time for things to change - okay, it will take a few years, but it is right that the picture may change. Again: cause and effect!

I have been working with telecom companies in Brazil since 2.000 or so, when the privatization process began. Today it seems an inevitable scenario of low quality. But the truth is that this scenario was not built overnight. It was so much activation that the client did not participate in the construction of anything. He became a passive spectator of all this. **The industry has created a market dependent on promotions and an arm wrestling to be able to break the subsidies of cell phones**. It would be easy at this moment to say that only companies and entrepreneurs in this sector are responsible for the poor quality of the relationship. But the truth is that we are inside this immense place, common to all of us, called planet Earth.

It is extremely pleasant to ask for and receive discounts. But act so the price be fair, gives a lot more work. According to a survey by the Akatu Institute, there is a concern, albeit small, with more conscious and sustainable forms of consumption and avoidance from harmful practices of doing business. But in practice, almost no real action on the part of consumers. This shows a distortion of the feminine principle (or acceptance), that is to say: **what is available is consumed without requiring any change**.

Only when consumers and businesses owners begin to realize the effect of their daily buying and selling actions does the market have a real chance for change, which can lead to better-quality relationship - and, of course, more conscious.

8 - IF THE RELANTIONSHIP IS REAL, SO HOW TO PERCEIVE IT

IF relationships were simple and objective subjects, we probably would not have any kind of conflict on the planet today. After all, only on documented human history, there are more than 5,000 years of wars, quarrels and all kind of disagreements. I know we have more time than this in the world, but this number seems to me a sufficient reference to understand that this is a challenging theme for all of us.

Apart from extreme cases, **most people seek happiness in relationships**. But if in most cases people (and businesses) enter on a relationship to be happy, the question then comes: what happens in the middle of the road with them to give up? It is somewhat challenging to do the following placement, but I have realized **that emotional maturity (personal or in business) is one of the first references of this happiness**.

If the customer expects happiness to happen only when he buys a certain product he needs or wants, then, of course, happiness will only be realized a second time if this product is consumed again, and again, and again... Similarly, for a company, if the achievement is only about winning new customers, then acquisition will always be the call of the day. On the other hand, considering that what happens outside (the actions) of people and companies has only relative impact overall (the emotions), indicates emotional maturity.

Take the case of great entrepreneurs who have succeeded in their trajectories. I have read and personally encountered several and various testimonials from people considered to be "successful". In all cases, two factors are always repeated: **these people do what they like** and, **despite all difficulties, they continue to persist**. Looking at relationships, my view is that moving on (despite difficulties) means that we *will work on it "no matter what," because we believe that the key to success lies inside, not outside*. On the other hand, unhappiness lies in one who has an opposite, naive even vision, I would say: that "I will only be happy (as a person or company) if I have what I want". That seems a childish point of view.

_____||_____

CONSIDERING THAT WHAT HAPPENS OUTSIDE (THE ACTIONS) OF PEOPLE AND COMPANIES HAS ONLY RELATIVE IMPACT OVERSALL (THE EMOTIONS), INDICATES EMOTIONAL MATURITY

_____||_____

Something that intrigues me is how some people (and their companies) do primarily what they like and still have their wallets full of money. My guess is that *to create a successful relationship, it is necessary for both sides to feel fulfilled*. It's no use doing what you do not like just because the customer wants it. Yes, serving the customer well is in the best relationship manuals, but that does not mean doing what the customer wants at any price. *It is also necessary to give him back his responsibility for the relationship*.

And if stones will come in the way, then it is better to know what they are. The first stone is to mistakenly consider happiness to be outside. It is trying to build a relationship through domination. It is to choose the ball, the field, the two teams and the judge, before starting the game. It is trying to take all the uncertainties out of the way and ensure that the outcome will be as expected. Because *the basic assumption of a relationship is precisely the uncertainty: that of discovering at any given moment another universe - the other*.

And in a relationship, inevitably comes the moment when we discover that we *actually have no control over each other*. It is a challenging point and yes, sometimes it is very difficult... The customer calls when we do not want, he asks for what we are not prepared to offer, and in the end still complains! What about the company? Promises what cannot fulfill, delivers a product less than expected, delay in delivery. Stones on the way...

The second stone is the other side of the same coin. It is giving up control and bringing all responsibility to you. It is to seek **ABSOLUTE** perfection. It is the intolerance to any kind of mistake. It is the thought of "if as a company I am perfect, then the customer will love me. He will buy what I'm offering. He will not even question. " Let's adjust things: I'm not talking here about a desire to overcome one's limits. From the desire to offer the other (the customer) the best we can. But it is a *desire starting from an exchange*. I do my best and then you must love me. In any situation, who wants a love like that?

Relationship presupposes imperfection, so that we all become more relaxed, on both sides: companies and all the people who relate to it. Everything in this case is imperfect. **Perfection comes from seeking, not from approaching**. And this I would say is a hard stone to withdraw from the path. After all, how many companies feel calm enough to look at themselves with such attention?

I have been observing that one way to remove this stone is to let the other be the way it is or want to be. It means real freedom. If the customer does not read the printed material that we send along with the product and then opens a ticket in the consumer's service because he did not feel informed, if he is unfair, he complains with no real justification; No matter the reason: we accept things as they are. **And accepting means not reacting**. Again: I am not saying that we should be passive. But perhaps peaceful, from the point of view of accepting what is, as it is. And this acceptance opens the door to real action. An assertive act. **BEING PRESENT**.

If, for example, customers do not pay, it does not mean that we will ignore this, as it is something that can lead the company to close. And then, nobody wins. But perhaps we must recognize, yes, that we have a problem of collecting, of cash. Customers do not pay. Otherwise, if the problem is directed at the client, the easiest would be to arm the largest collection guerrilla. Letters and more letters, one SMS every 30 seconds, send all the bad payers information to lower their credit score, in short, just "re-act".

Acting, on the other hand, can be extremely different. Recognizing that we have a collecting problem and looking honestly and deeply into it, we can identify that the company is not selling to the right audience; that maybe is giving credit when it should not; that the products have low quality and the customers' natural reaction may be not to pay. That is, the **focus changes from the outside in. The problem may still be in the client, but it is no longer him**.

To close this chapter, I would say that an excellent tool is control. Not external control, but **self-control**. It is to stop reacting on relationships. It's starting to just act. It is to consider what we have of tools in hand now and what would be the best way for everyone to go up one more step: the company, its clients and the relationship between them.

9 - HOW TO BE STRONG ENOUGH TO 'SUSTAIN' THE RELATIONSHIP

A few years ago, I had the rare opportunity to participate in the conception of the company's mission that I had begun some years earlier. As it was a small team, we had the participation of literally the entire company. The process was facilitated by a professional who, by my perception, had not planned to close the work of about a year, in the way it ended. It was the last of three meetings that were scheduled with the entire team.

I have the impression that this was somehow a magical moment. One of those rare moments where life changes its course before our eyes. After a few comings and goings, the phrase that would be the basis of our work from then on, began to take shape. I have no reference to how long it took, but it must have been between two and three hours of hard work.

In the end, I felt a heavy weight on my shoulders. The facilitator asked directly to everyone: "Is this the mission of the company?" And read the sentence that had just been completed. He then looked at me and asked, "Do you agree?". A long silence afterwards, I turned the question back to the people who were present: "Is this what we all want? ".

It was a rather strange dialogue, but I realized that at that moment I had a choice. Just like everyone else there. A conscious choice on the way forward. I noticed, however, that the only choice I had was to accept the challenge. The choice of what to do was no longer mine. My role was only to serve something that was already set. There was only one thing to do. Or not!

Two or three years after that day, one of the team members who was present at that time, came to me and said, "I think the company is not going the way we would like, you need to look at it! ". So I realized that, rather than having good managerial skills, leader and relationship qualities with people, someone who chooses to lead is serving others, everyone involved: their clients, their employees, society and shareholders. When a company chooses to serve only one of these groups in isolation, leaving the others out, the "undock" begins. I do not tell this story out of presumption or pride, just to bring a personal example of the importance that **LEADING IS SERVING**.

A leader must be willing to support something. Regardless of the challenge and the difficulties, it is the choice to keep alive the "flame" that makes people's lives better every day. Many winds and much water will fall on this flame. Some will even try to put it out. It's up to the leader to keep it on. I also noticed that **the larger the company (or the government, if we want to look more broadly) the greater the**

seduction of power for those who lead. It creates the false impression that you are being served. After all, you become Mr. / Mrs. President, and the pampering begins.

There are still rare cases of companies and governments that have the clarity that they are serving their clients and led. A friend of mine says, with some conviction, that companies that do not serve society should close. And based on that, I go on...

Within the roller coaster of emotions that is having a business open to the public, things only work daily because someone (or "somebody") puts energy every day for the company to go forward. Be it energy from the money of the client or investors, from the work and from the personal and intellectual effort of the people, and so forth. The great challenge, though, is how to properly direct all that energy. Taking this theme to the personal level, yoga (a technique whose purpose is to connect its practitioner with the Whole) has the function (besides other deeper issues) of allowing the yogi (the practitioner of this ancient technique) to know how to control your own life energy. And if at the individual level this is so challenging that it can take many, many years, and still not get very far, imagine on a broader level. Proof of this is that today we have a planet that suffers because its "residents" have no idea how to properly manage their resources!

We come here to an important point, and that requires attention. I began to realize that the energy that moves the building is the same one that drives the destruction. **The energy that moves a good relationship and union is the same that moves separation**. It seemed a little strange to me, but I began to realize that we are talking about choices here. The curious thing is that this directing of energy does not happen at random, nor does it consciously in all situations. There is a very, very delicate point here: the connection of creative energy with negative situations. I explain. When the person on our team said, "We are not heading in the right direction," she was signaling that our energy was being put into something contrary to what we had defined. If our proposal was to serve our client well, perhaps this was not happening at that time.

So, **how do you improve the Relationship inside and outside the company**? Some key points:

IT IS VITAL THAT THERE IS A SPONSOR.
> Someone (who may be a single person or a small group of leaders) who consciously decides to support the idea of a better relationship. If the relationship is not going well, it is fact that the energy is connected with something that is dragging it from the company. It may be, for

example, anger and misunderstanding of not doing the best that you know is possible. It is therefore necessary to bring about to consciousness what is not going well.

IT'S REQUIRED SOME COURAGE IN ACCEPTING THINGS TO BE RIGHT!

Sounds weird? But unfortunately, it is very common. You may know people who are afraid of success and happiness. Someone who lives talking about how things go wrong every day and how many problems there are. Your energy is directed to the problem, not to the solution. It is then necessary to re-channeling this energy, and accept that something can work! "And if the customer is happy and smiling at me, what should I do? "

IT'S ALSO NEEDED TO ACCEPT THAT THINGS WILL NOT BE PERFECT.

This is an imperfect world. Having a good relationship means improving every day, and not being perfect today and always. It is first a decision, and then a daily effort.

THEREFORE, THE DECISIONS MUST BE BREAKED UP BY MINOR PARTIES.

Do not be tempted to try to change everything now. While someone holds the decision that the relationship needs to improve, others are working on it on different fronts. The change starts in and is gradually shifting away. Therefore, plant seeds of improvement, protect them, and expect them to thrive...

LOOK DAILY TO "RE-CONNECT" THE VITAL ENERGY OF THE BUSINESS WITH THE ESSENCE OF YOUR COMPANY.

It could be something simple, like: "let's re-train our employees again about how to make the best coffee we can deliver to our customers." It is to love what you are doing now, and to do with love that which presents itself. Simple but effective!

10 - "WHAT IF MY PAST CONDEMNS ME?"

IF you've opened a new business, you know the challenges of making your first sales. However, dedicated and caring one may be to do something new and beautiful, this is not always recognized in the same way as the founder of the company sees. A nascent company is like a child, it needs care and attention, both on the part of the one who created it and the society in which it is inserted. It does not startle the death rate of companies in the first five to ten years for ignoring this fact.

Just like a child, a young company needs basic care: food (financial income), attention (internal and external support), some simple rules of coexistence (legal and functional organization), and something I see as essential, freedom of expression. As a baby that grows, the company will start walking, running, falling, sometimes getting hurt and again walking again. And it is during this journey that some seeds are planted. Some of love, and some of pain. And it is precisely the seeds of pain that, as the company begins to really grow, come to the surface. Because, the past that has not been integrated, that is, that did not result in lessons, it is not possible to be forgotten.

And how do these seeds of pain come to the surface? Imagine for a moment the following situation: the person buys a dog and every day comes home and whacks the pussy - and, no, for

God's sake, do not do it at home! (That guy, Pavlov, has done enough strange things in the name of science.) Even without doing this crazy test, it is possible to know that one expects two natural reactions from the poor dog: an uncontrolled fear when he sees the owner or, at some point, his will revolt, biting the person back.

Without making so much drama, suffice it to say that companies also suffer daily setbacks, which are leaving traces. It is the customer that does not pay, the supplier that does not deliver, the employee that does not comply. The company also generates its own marks. It promises something to customers and does not comply, offers a product that does "almost" (but not) everything the advertisement says. Either way, these "growth marks" stay there, somewhere in the heart of the business.

_____||_____

AS A CHILD, A YOUNG COMPANY NEEDS BASIC CARE: FOOD (FINANCIAL REVENUE), ATTENTION (INTERNAL AND EXTERNAL SUPPORT), SOME SIMPLE RULES OF COEXISTENCE (LEGAL AND FUNCTIONAL ORGANIZATION) AND, SOMETHING I SEE AS ESSENTIAL, FREEDOM OF EXPRESSION.

_____||_____

But know: even with all the difficulties, life always walks to the best. Therefore, the company and the society in which it is inserted will try to repair each of these marks. How? In your daily dealings! Each contact becomes not a better service, but a way to repair an account that has been left open. Whether on the client or on the company side.

However, until the awareness of these facts becomes apparent, it is like walking blind. Problems arise every day and we do not even know where to start. And I want to point out here that there are no victims. On neither side! If this is not addressed, in business and society (represented by people as consumers), we will not have an evolution.

Are you thinking I'm overreacting? For there is an American documentary that tells in detail how some cities in the United States organized to prevent large retailers from setting up stores in the city after it became apparent that the entrance of some stores was ending local commerce. Without making any kind of judgment - whether that is good or not - the fact is **that people have realized that companies should serve their customers, not vice versa. And because of this they mobilized**.

I have seen more than once references that if half of the best-known brands were out of the market overnight, no one would complain. This points out that **the importance that companies give to themselves is totally** *disconnected from reality*. Sounds like a dead end? Take a breath, there is a way out.

The first step is to face the daily problems as signs that something is being asked to be looked at, avoiding the search for guilty and the so famous witch hunt. The second step is to look at the anger, anxiety and resentment that will naturally arise - believe me, find out at the end of the month that a "smart" customer called your call center on the weekend of the cell phone and left the line hanging by 48 Hours just to receive credits from his operator in the prepaid is not very easy to swallow!

The next layer to be hit is the layer where that seed of pain sprouts... From the past it comes out and says to you: "I tried to offer my product in the best way and that's how the customer repaid after so many years of relationship? ". Here, it is worth taking special care: *Do not enter into the seductive way of finding that there are "good customers" and "bad customers"*. Yes, this may even be a truth (and probably it is), but if you use it, this will suffice to justify the problems for some time, do nothing, and after that see them return stronger. So, understand: *If your customer service is bad, this holds true for both the "good" and the "bad" customers*.

Here is the problem-question: "If I willingly accepted everything, even if with some difficulty, why is the problem in the relationship with the client remaining? ". Honestly, I do not have the definitive answer, but I have a question that I have seen open a world of possibilities: "despite all this difficulty and the knowledge of all the defects of your customers, yours (as a company) and everything else, ***still would you offer your best to your client?***"

I admit that this is one of the most challenging questions I've ever faced. But one guy named Steve Jobs, in a meeting with the world's largest record companies, had to face it. It happened somewhat like this: "Steve, are you telling us to sell our music at a price far below the price at which we sell a CD? Are you still telling us to leave these songs in an open format so that people can pass on to all their friends, even after Napster has almost finished with our industry? ".
The answer? "Yes, because I believe that maybe 20% of people do not give a damn about copyright, and they will continue to download songs for free - which, however much they try, you will not be able to stop. But I also believe that 80% of people certainly want to buy music legally and sleep peacefully. The only problem is that this is not available today on an industrial and organized scale. "

Luckily, dear Steve was right. As I finish writing this chapter, I hear songs I have been able to buy online thanks to his courage and attitude.

11 - HOW TO 'SOLVE' IT IF BECOMES TOO 'HEAVY'

THE proximity between what happens in our personal relationships and in the relationships, we have with brands seems so great that some terms refer to an exclusive feeling for passionate couples. I speak of something so natural and eventually so ignored, that it is **THE NEED TO FEEL BELOVED**.

Bringing this concept to brand's arena means, *being chosen even though you are the most expensive product or service in the list of options*. It is when the client chooses us without being able to give a rational justification. **EMOTION**, **REASON** and **POCKET** begin to have a balanced weight with each other.

In the "infancy" of a company, the recognition of this desire is extremely apparent. Countless stories of entrepreneurs have gone out door to door to present their brands until they become known... and beloved. But even after the company grows and flourishes, this need to receive attention remains. After all, we would like to receive as much attention as we feel our competitors are.

Do you see yourself in this situation? Watch out! This is the beginning of a dangerous journey. Because when we begin to realize that our brand may not be as much loved as we think it should, *we may fall into the error of seeking external references to replace the eventual "pain" of not being loved or chosen.*

Certainly, it is easier to justify that "the 'sky' is falling", "the consumer has changed", "the credit lines are more restrictive". Yes, all this may be true, and it has natural influence. But compared to the challenge of setting up a new brand, this is basically child's play. Let the great entrepreneurs say it!

The truth is that it is somewhat painful to accept the fact that we would like to be the chosen brand, but eventually this may not happen. Thus, one proceeds to seek some external substitute as justification, a search that can be extremely subtle. It can happen even before the first signs of "no-choice" are apparent.

Without making any kind of judgment on recognized market indicators - such as Market Share, Share of Wallet, Top of Mind, and so on - I need to say that route deviation begins when these external indicators become the guide, not the reference. Yes, it is important to know in what situation we are as a brand. It is important to know how people who work in the same market are. **The problem is when the market becomes a group of numbers and graphs and stops reflecting the people who form it.** I would say the poison is "trying to fit in". It's starting to do things based on the competition or other external reference, leaving aside, without realizing it, someone who was important in the past: the customer!

The **FIRST STEP** to retake the pulse is to be aware that, yes, it can be painful not to be chosen at that moment. It is only after that that we begin to have some references of what can be happening "at home". It is also possible to have a positive result for some time with actions not very connected to the brand, only in the direction of reacting to an external identification, such as the drop-in sales of a product. Of course, promotions work, and will always work. Eventually we forget that they are temporary and show a decreasing outcome over time.

The success of a brand is only true when it positively impacts people's lives. I do not mean here just a customer satisfaction survey. The question for the customer is: "where does our product or service or even the fact that our brand is close to you make your life better? ". **This is what really matters: what a brand is adding value to people**.

The possibility that opens with this is that the brand starts to do things no longer waiting for a recognition - because it is almost impossible to know exactly what people expect from us as a brand. This is changeable and difficult to put into words. But the only true recognition is that which is received for free. We do what needs to be done simply because this is the best thing to do, not because someone is asking or will bring some sort of guaranteed recognition in the end. This is **INTEGRITY**.

While it is still painful not to be the chosen brand in some situations, we begin to do things based on the heart of the company. That which mobilizes people to do their best daily.

The **SECOND STEP** in this journey is to give the customer freedom so that he can eventually not choose us. In a relationship that works, there must be freedom on both sides. The question for a company is: even if some customers do not like your products or even say bad things of your brand, will your attitude remain the same in a positive way?

The question seems strange, but a well-known American retail brand makes the exchange or refund of the products without question. The most famous case came from a customer who was reimbursed for a product he had never bought at the store. Whoever told this was not the store, but the customer himself, who subsequently apologized publicly, because he had been wrong. He told how he found the attitude of the admirable brand by exchanging a product that did not belong to them, just because he said he was sure he had bought there.

I have the impression that ***many of the difficulties that arise come from the lack of objectivity for something that is essentially subjective***: the relationship itself. Sometimes it lacks a bit of clarity and openness to admit, for example, that the relationship is in bad shape. And only this objectivity can bring the next step in the relationship.

I begin to realize that brands that have a good relationship with their audience have some characteristics that are worth looking at more closely. These companies:

> ❯ Are allowed not to be loved and chosen, which opens the door for them to recognize their own value, and also helps not to create subterfuges to be chosen. Typically, they are brands that do less promotions than their peers;

> ❯ Do not try to control the relationship, but have the humility to know that the customer can choose another brand if they want;

> ❯ They look at the relationship objectively: if it's okay, that's fine; If it is not, let's not mask the situation. This kind of attitude opens-up the opportunity to do what

needs to be done, and no longer what is supposed to be done;

❯ They look at external indicators as indicators of how they are and as a reference for improvement, but not as guidelines. This means that they can take unpopular attitudes, but they are the best thing to do at a given moment;

❯ If they were people, I would say they have a **MATURE** personality. They act calmly even in adverse conditions. "It's all part of a passing game, good times and bad times. In the end, it is our internal attitude that will tell us how we are doing, "they think; And act correctly.

Well, at this point in the game you might be thinking something like, "I think that customer relationship is not for me. It gives a lot more work than I had thought... ". Yes, it may be true. It is likely to work harder than most people realize. After all, if you pick up between ten and twenty people close by, how many do you know they have been married for over 15 years? And if in personal relationships, where there is typically a formal commitment, this permanence does not happen, what will be the relationship between business and customers, where there is usually no formal agreement?

So, what to do when the company realizes that? Yes, there is a lot of work ahead? One piece of advice I can give you is: choose to do things that bring inner satisfaction. Maybe launch a **remake** of a product that has been successful in the past. Not for the expectation of financial return, but for the simple joy of remembering good moments. In a relationship of two, this "recall" of the past sometimes helps to alleviate the tension of the present moment, and to open a window of reconciliation and mutual growth.

12 - FROM NOW ON

IF there is a chapter more difficult than the others, I would say it is this one, because it is necessary to have objectivity! And being **OBJECTIVE** means talking the truth clearly and transparently. I'm not telling here as something known as brutal truth, which is to speak the truth at any cost, without measuring the consequences, with the simple goal of taking the momentary emotional discomfort out of you. The truth is intolerant... but patient! Subjectivity, on the other hand, comes from a "nuanced" truth, a half-truth, an omission or even a lie.

I choose here to start from the end to the beginning: to reach objectivity demands **CHOICE** and **COURAGE**. *Choice* to build better relationships and *courage* to move on and act, no matter what you discover along the way.

The **FIRST STEP** is to know that we will open space to consider that the company may be wrong about the way it relates with the people in the relationship: whether customers, employees, suppliers or anyone else. Then comes the *choice*. And, in that case, choice means a **STRATEGIC PLANNING**. There is, of course, a myriad of techniques and tools to do this. But what I would like you, reader, to keep in mind, is that the clearer your destination, the easier it will be to go through difficulties (and they will certainly come).

Subjectivity to a company, by contrast, may be to consider the customer as **we think** he is. He is like someone who, when putting on a pair of glasses, thinks that he started to see people not only more clearly but inside them. We must know that there is something more powerful than the glasses we are using. A Database Marketing (or the brand new Big Data), for example, helps a lot to refine the true vision of the customer. It looks like the x-ray to our vision: it goes beyond the sharpness that the glasses give. And ignoring it, pretending that only the glasses have made us see completely, can disrupt the correct view. Here's an example:

Until a few years ago, a person who was registered within a credit service protection had his name permanently tainted. But some entrepreneurs have identified that in many cases this situation was momentary. They made room for doubt and began to realize that some of these people "**has been**" momentarily defaulters. They went on to consider that, even with the credit being denied, some customers deserved credit for making new purchases. Over time, this proved to be assertive and gave rise to new commercial strategies.

This step of strategic planning (or choice, if you prefer) is quite important. **It is to have the clarity of where we are in fact at a specific moment**.

Returning to objectivity; Yes, some customers remained defaulted, or even identified that there were cases of fraud. But having considered that all people were equal (subjectivity), left buried for a long time the opportunity of new business. **With this model of objectivity, however, we begin to differentiate what are facts and what are perceptions**.

Lack of objectivity to look at the client and the relationship is usually tainted by two factors:

> **RIGOR** - which means a "binary" view: the customer is this or that. This is what, in my opinion, leads many professionals to basic mistakes, such as considering, for example, that the fact that a person likes to "enjoy" the company page means that he is a customer always and forever. People are branded customers enough to have their needs met;

> **IDEALIZATION** – Which means that the client is what we would like him to be. It leads to thoughts such as: "our customer is more loyal than the competition"; "Our customer pays on time"; And so on. Yes, some customers are more loyal to your brand than others. Some customers are up-to-date... and some are not. Again, a database support can greatly help you put

the concepts and biases in their proper places.

This "thick view" about who really is the person with whom the company relates has two reasons to go:

1. **PROUD**: "Our client cannot have defects. After all, the defects of our customers will be associated with our brand! ";

2. **INSECURITY**: "If the customer is not what I want him to be, then where we are going to? "

The danger is to navigate between two extremes: to completely ignore the defects (and the virtues) or to be extremely harsh in the judgment.

Finding out that people who are close to the company are not what they idealized, be it your internal or external audience, it is eventually delicate. And this discomfort comes not so much in the discovery, but in the moment in which the company realizes chosen simple glasses to see the reality, when it could have resorted to an x-ray.

Having done all this analysis, you can give the **SECOND STEP**, which is **to start to see people - inside and outside the company - as they are, with their faults and virtues**, and not as we would like them to be.

Do not rush, this ability to get through turbulent waters comes with time. It is like a relationship between two people who fall in love: in the beginning, everything is heaven. Then comes the storms. But at last one begins to learn that, in addition to all the difficulties and challenges in the relationship, there is a lotus flower, which deserves to be watered and preserved.

13 - HOW TO PREPARE YOURSELF TO THE END

YES, like everything else in life, relationships are finite. But what is the end of the relationship? Or rather, **WHEN** does the end of the relationship between a company and its customer happen? I'm not talking here about that stage in the relationship with the customer in which the company considers it still able to fall into the category of so-called win-back or recovery / reactivation. I´m dealing here with that moment from which it is no longer possible to return to an earlier stage.

Seeking a practical example, it is that day when the writer tells the company that he was selling typewriters (maybe you, younger reader no longer has the reference of what this is, so I suggest you search the internet): "you were my favorite so far. I never chose another brand or model, but the world has changed. I now write on computers. I even see a certain romanticism in tightening the old keys, but even my publisher does not accept the originals on paper anymore."

This is a profoundly challenging moment, which we could call "*the great unknown*".

Recently a friend told me that a customer who accounted for 35% of his company's revenue simply reduced his spending to 10% of his monthly bill. Some strategists would say: "But how did the company accumulate such a high percentage in a single customer? "; "Let's set up a portfolio strategy"; "We are going to reduce the number of employees in the same proportion", and so on... Without ignoring how much a strategy can do for a company, all these alternatives may be valid, but that is not what I am dealing with here. I speak of the delicate challenge of accepting that things have arrived (or will one day come) to their end.

To avoid accepting that every relationship will inevitably one day come to an end is to pretend that one does not have to face the fact that one day, sooner or later, things will be different than they are today. It's almost a paradox, I know. How do you stay firm in your company's current strategy and at the same time have the lightness to change course at the same time? Going straight to the point: being realistic with the **beginning, the middle and the end**.

It is, as a company, a confrontation with itself. It is to know that what the company does today may not be doing tomorrow. It is accepting that conscious choice of customer relationship will be like a compass to guide your direction. With this compass, the company will always have the choice to follow or not in that direction, but it can no longer avoid knowing that the customer has changed or is changing. It is having the courage to bring this end of the relationship into everyday life. It is to have, as a marketer, to wake up every morning and say to himself, "I know everything I could know about my client until yesterday, but today is a new day. It's a new opportunity to learn deeper into who he is, what he needs, how my company can contribute to him... **TODAY**! ".

It is to consider the customer, first as a person, vivid and changeable. And look at that person as a universe to be unraveled daily. It's never say, "I know everything! ".

Nonsense what do I say? Ask photographers who thought digital photography was second-rate, not enough quality for the customer to trade something tangible and real like a paper for files on a hard drive. At the time, maybe even the customer had such clarity. But the "never" turned the present moment.

If you are still with me, maybe it's time to look a step further in the relationship. Because, after all, **relationships are also a study about yourself**. About what the company does and for whom it does. Opening the door to the relationship is walking first through unknown terrain, where there are no right or wrong answers, and discovering that there are some barriers along the way.

The first of these barriers **is to be aware that there are situations that the company itself decides not to see**. It is choosing to ignore that buying at a very low cost may be generating at the other end underemployment or an unregulated extraction of resources.

The second barrier is **the natural rejection of a closer relationship with the client**. Because, after all, it is easy to set up a call center to keep the voice of the customer away from the company, and often necessary for the company to breathe; But letting that remain so is like killing the messenger because he does not bring good news.

The third barrier is **the realization that things have a greater connection than we can realize**. It is to think that we are isolated in our market, in our country, in our continent...

Want to better understand what I just said? Stop reading for a moment and look around; Then try to realize how many things came from within a radius of 100 miles from where you are now. Probably few, right? **What every entrepreneur and every company (in the sum of the people who work there) seeks is the true expression of oneself**. It is to be able to put into practice what we love and know best.

And we're still far from it. The proof: such is the madness that we get in our daily life that authors such as Domenico De Masi wrote about "Creative Idleness", the importance of stopping from time to time so we can do what we really like. It made me ask, "So, what are we doing daily? Is that what we do not like?!!! ". Better stop before it's too late...

If we are talking more about what is inside than what is outside, i.e. the client as a reflection of ourselves, then it is time to look at the internal obstacles, which are within us and often we do not want to see. **To decide to see and to overcome them is the way to go in search of a better expression of ourselves and therefore of the other**.

The first of these internal obstacles is **PRIDE**. Pride is the first major obstacle that inhibits the possibility of recognizing which points within the company can be improved. After all, who wants to look in the mirror and see a crooked image. It's one thing to read the call center reports and make excuses that points to customer failures, of how he does not understand what we're doing. But it is another thing to listen to complaints without criticism and to separate what is true from what is not. Maybe the customer is wrong in something, yes; But if this bothers us as a company, then there is still something to be looked at and improved on.

The second obstacle is the natural resistance of the human being to changes, or what we might call **PERSONAL WILL**. The world changes every minute, but we try to create a world of make-believe, in which everything remains the same forever. Worse, the personal will is a natural resistance when it comes to change. After all, if the company begins to become aware of the impact that it has been generating so far in the relationship and ultimately in the client, who wants to take on such trouble?

The third and last obstacle is natural fear. **THE FEAR OF THE UNKNOWN**. Overcoming fear is the next step in the relationship. It is to follow without the guarantee that everything will be as planned and expected. It is the "middle" of the relationship. It is to know that we do not know everything. It is surrendering to something that is beyond rationality. The relationship with the client cannot be fully explained in spreadsheets and calculations. One part of it can, but another part is based on trust. It is the opening for lightness.

No, it's not easy, I'll admit. But who said relationship is a simple thing?

The true relationship between company and client (as so many others in life) is an experience of humility. I think one of the biggest examples I've seen about it was Steve Jobs' decision to lower the price of the iPod just hours before launching the product. For me it was the recognition that "okay, we went wrong, all the spreadsheets we did, calculations and research, studies and everything else was wrong, or at least 'not so accurate.' Our client is here on the street in front of me, but he's not the same person we thought he was when we were in the office. We need to make a correction. Now! ".

How many companies would have the humility and courage to make such a decision?

14 - HOW TO DANCE WITH LIGHTNESS

ALMOST at the end of the book, I conclude that a good relationship (whether it is between company and clients, employees, suppliers, government, society, etc.) is at the same time a walk out and a walk in. It is a discovery of the world outside and the world inside.

To look only inwardly is to create an "ego-centric" enterprise, centered around itself, its problems and its needs, without understanding its impact on society. Just looking out, is to create an "ec-centric" company, which lives on the basis only of external opinions, surveys, market potential readings, awards or external indicators of success, losing perspective on itself.

Giving my own vision, I would say that the best point is **the one in which the outer and the inner touch each other**. It is the moment when the company seeks in the first place a good relationship with its customers (after all, it is for them ultimately that the products and services will be delivered), but at the same time respects itself. Know its own skills and abilities. All of this, of course, can change over time - after all, **the only constant in the world is change** - but the company has some clarity about its role in the world. Whether in its locality, state, or country.

If at this point you have any difficulty in knowing where to start or in which direction to go in the relationship with your clients, just look for a positive legacy. This is what the Orientals call "positive karma" or "karma that frees oneself. "

For this initial reference of the company that we want to be, let's take an example. Imagine a German company that came to produce decorative papers in Brazil. It will, very quickly, have some accessible references to build upon. Looking at Germany, could bring: precision, durability, persistence to produce the best. Looking at Brazil, it could include natural beauty, human warmth and the exclusivity of our fauna and flora. And, adding all these references, we would have such a beautiful and precise role that it would imitate the design and grooves of a Brazilian millenarian tree, but without the need to reduce an inch of our native forests. What's more, at a distance, people would say it's a perfect piece of hardwood!

This is the beauty of self-knowledge. It is knowing where we are and what this can contribute to us. Looking at that Cherokee tale of the two wolves is to feed the Good Wolf. While we have our positive references, we must also have the clarity that the Creator is, after all, someone creative! Decided to put inside of each of us the Good and the Evil. Or do you think that this American tale came from nowhere?

It is to begin to understand that - without any judgment - evil is that zero-sum social game... or less. It is to build a model of production and consumption in which one always loses. While good is the understanding that we are all part of the same Whole. It is to understand that when one loses, everyone loses.

To cite a personal example, stopped in traffic inside a taxi the other day, I saw a graffiti on the wall that said: "**You ARE the traffic**". A simple sentence, but that brought me a deep reflection. After all, if I am in traffic, I am also THE traffic!

I could go into this last chapter for at least another four or five pages. But I preferred to end with two advices that I can give from my own learning when talking about relationships.

The first is the need for **SELF-KNOWLEDGE**. I think a good quote from this is the movie **Matrix**, in which there is a moment that, for me, illustrates this very well. It is that scene in which Neo (the main actor) interacts with the Oracle. The camera then points to a phrase that is above his head: "Know thyself." This is the key. *Self-knowledge for me is the "tool" that enables one to understand the other from within himself*. It's like a "shortcut" to the perfect relationship.

The second is **ABILITY** - I would call it even mastery - to **know how to balance what goes on inside and what happens outside**. Quoting Steve again (Jobs, of course), I think in his own way he knew, mutually, take advantage of and ignore what was going on around him.

I close this book giving a warm thank you for coming here with me. And wishing you sincerely relationships that extend your life and your perception.

Namasté!

BEFORE WE GO

"JUST BEFORE we say goodbye, I would like to reinforce my invitation so that we remain connected in some way. I leave below my main channels of interaction:

- **Blog at Exame.com** - http://exame.abril.com.br/blog/relacionamento-antes-do-marketing/ - que escrevo semanalmente juntamente com meu sócio Marcio Oliveira

- **Linked-in** - www.linkedin.com/in/lbarci/

- www.youdb.com.br – **youDb's** website, company I founded, with the aim of contributing to a better relationship between Companies and Clients

- www.facebook.com/youDb/ - **youDb's Facebook page**

Leonardo Barci
leonardo@barci.com.br

The Marketing Relationship Agency

This book was sponsored by **youDb**, a company that seeks, through the ability to bring reason and emotion together, to help companies build sustainable, healthy, measurable and lasting relationships among all people involved in the business: customers, employees, shareholders and the community. To know how to put into practice the contents and learning brought by the author, contact:

www.youdb.com.br
contato@youdb.com.br
+55 11 3078.3203
R Florida 1758– 11 andar – São Paulo – SP - 01418-904 - Brazil

MIND THE GAP – BECAUSE THE RELATIONSHIP WITH CUSTOMERS COMES FIRST

In this book, both fun and lightly technical, you will find the way to think and rethink the market and its marketing performance, in a text that brings together romance, theoretical support and some practical references.

Written for marketing people by profession or by passion, who chose this area of knowledge as a form of expression.

49 REFLECTIONS ON MARKETING & BUSINESS

    A few years ago, I started getting annoyed and wondering how to work with marketing and communication. My questioning is mainly based on how much these activities are collaborating to increase what I call THE GAP between what a company says it is (or wants to be) and its actual daily practice in the relationship with its clients.

    Since then, I've decided to record a few phrases and thoughts that came naturally from chats, meetings, projects, and what I call "cafeteria reflections."

    The purpose of this book is to share 49 of these phrases and reflections, which bring a lot about my vision of marketing, relationship and business.

    And why 49? Simply because 50 would be too obvious.

www.ingramcontent.com/pod-product-compliance
Lightning Source LLC
Chambersburg PA
CBHW052302220526
45471CB00001B/447